Copyright © 2022 by (Donald K. Morgan)
All Rights Reserved.
No part of this book may be used or reproduced by any means, graphic, electronic, or mechanical, including photocopying, recording, taping, or by any information storage retrieval system without the written permission of the publisher.

THE PRINCIPLES OF BUSINESS:

5 principles of business every Manager should know.

By
Donald K. Morgan

Table of content
Introduction
Chapter 1
Principle of vision
Chapter 2
Principle of Discernment
Chapter 3
Principle of Leadership
Chapter 4
Principle of Reputation
Chapter 5
Principle of Consistency

INTRODUCTION

The fundamental rules that are helpful for making decisions and resolving issues are known as business principles.
Any principle that provides helpful instructions in a wide range of interactions and processes is frequently implemented by departments, teams, and organizations. The Principles allow managers and business owners the ability to choose what has to be done to complete specified tasks and to deal with problems that may emerge in management. Managers and business owners become more effective by following these guidelines.

Chapter 1

Principle of Vision

Vision impels your business forward. Without vision, an organization needs heading and meanders randomly with no route or methodologies to arrive at their objective. This absence of vision cultivates a climate that heedlessly takes business that comes to them — regardless of whether it is some unacceptable kind of business — rather than forcefully searching out business that their center abilities would best serve. Of vision gets a business in the place of shortcoming rather than strength.

With vision, everything is conceivable. Vision rouses imagination, lights reason and advancement, and encourages development. It gives a plan and permits a business to remain focused and have a check to quantify your advancement appropriately.

Vision alongside an organization's central goal, reason, values, and fundamental belief are the groundwork of each and every business. Similarly as a house can't be worked without an establishment and diagram, neither can a business.

Without clear vision:
- Irregularity in work item or administration
- Stagnation
- Diminished income and benefits
- Loss of clients
- High representative turnover
- Elevated degree of disarray
- Unfortunate client assistance
- No genuine course or targets to meet
- Persistently resolving similar issues
- Most time is spent on extinguishing fires
- Constantly employing some unacceptable individuals
- Inefficient correspondence
- Absence of administration and responsibility

With clear vision:
- Consistency in work item or administration
- Development
- Productivity
- Expansion in ideal clients
- Client maintenance
- Wealth of references
- Design and request
- Time to deal with business and systems
- Vital targets being set and met
- Strategies and methodology set up
- Grant winning client assistance

Positions being filled by the ideal individuals
Low worker turnover
Useful and successful correspondence
Elevated degree of authority and responsibility
A business that has a vision, realizes its destination on time.

Chapter 2
Principle of Discernment (Perception)

Client discernment alludes to the client's assessment of your business or items. It sums up how clients feel about your image including each immediate or roundabout experience they've had with your organization. By observing client insight, your organizations can detect normal client trouble spots and further develop the client venture. Discernment is staggeringly significant in business. Could it be said that you are seen as modest and dreadful or selective and costly? Is it true that you are seen as a specialist and experienced or a beginner who has no clue about the thing you're doing?

Insight holds a lot more profound significance than we can envision. It assumes an immense part in forming the manner in which we characterize and get things done

inside our public activity, our own life and without a doubt our business life. It is a critical part of business especially with regards to showcasing
 and investigating the different reasons of the significance of discernment in business:
1. Powerful discernment.
For a purchaser, it is vital to understand what they are putting into is worth the effort and for this, the business needs to showcase itself to demonstrate them right. Insight is reality. The business needs to ensure that they produce promotions that are adequately applicable to persuade the client. Now and again, organizations use duplicity or control to accomplish this, however normally get found out. We need to place out our most desirable characteristics introduce ourselves in the most ideal light.
 I said that discernment becomes reality. Allow me to make sense of. You have two experts. One is perfect at promoting and gives the impression of being the master. The other basically buckles down, perhaps is excellent (perhaps awesome) but since they hush up, don't showcase themselves well, the insight may not be that they are awesome. How this becomes the truth is that the one

with the incredible discernment gets more business, more experience and is more effective - in some measure monetarily. They are currently doing all around well and basically have become better in certain perspectives and subsequently, discernment has become reality.

2. Contacting the customers.

One of the key factors that impact the shopper discernment is the openness to the items. Normally, assuming a client has more information about a specific item and is happy with the data given, there is a higher opportunity for them to get it as opposed to purchasing something that they either haven't caught wind of or haven't seen at this point. This is where publicizing the contributions of a specific business becomes an integral factor. Instructing our clients is a significant part of showcasing, insight and successful selling.

3. Risk Perception.

Organizations should likewise think about the gamble discernment that clients might have while purchasing their items. The more hazardous a speculation is, the more troublesome it very well may be to get purchasers to act. Consequently, assurances and guarantees lessen that view of hazard, especially assuming the thing is costly or huge.

4. Clutching clients.

Finally, when a client has bought an item, it is the obligation of the business to ensure that they don't lose the client. This implies that the business should encourage discernment that will thus bring about productive ways of behaving for the business. The business should keep a decent standing and start brand unwaveringly. One method for doing this is by offering better client support as this assists with keeping up with the discernment that the business really focuses on its clients' advantages. Along these lines, the client creates dedication towards the business, making a consistent income stream subsequently making it more challenging for different organizations to remove these clients. The client needs to see they are esteemed and are being taken care of.

5. Industry Perceptions.

Frequently ventures or gatherings will cultivate an insight. For instance, a clinical expert you hope to stand by ages to see. Mentors have a standing of being costly (yet my starter bundle is truly reasonable), remove is frequently seen as undesirable (yet McDonalds have some incredible serving of mixed greens/sound decisions). Assuming your industry has a particular discernment, and that isn't true in your business, you want to teach your possibilities with regards to your place of distinction. Obviously some industry discernments are useful, for instance Certified Practicing Accountants (Cpa's) have a view of being qualified, experienced and educated.

Discernment has consistently assumed a significant part in business. Whenever applied and utilized appropriately it tends to be a significant key in aiding the business develop and make due on the lookout. It furnishes the business with a viewpoint that will assist it with thriving from here on out and foster driving business open doors too. What discernment would you say you are putting out there?

Customers should be able to have a good Perception regarding your business.

Chapter 3
Principle of Leadership

There are numerous initiative styles and speculations with respect to what elements make the best chiefs. The accompanying

initiative standards are ordinarily viewed as fundamental to a business achievement:
Show others how its done.
Initiative is about individuals.
Center around change.
Be human and concede botches.
Grasp the benefit of tuning in.
Foster authority abilities.
Advance variety.
Cooperate to accomplish more.
Have strong qualities.
Use innovation and advancement.
Help to foster future pioneers.

1. Show others how its done.

Numerous effective pioneers exhibit how to act, perform errands and take care of their responsibilities. A decent pioneer models brilliant way of behaving and should have the option to rouse and empower individuals. The best organizations and associations have pioneers who assist their staff with understanding the worth in their vision and show them how everybody can cooperate to accomplish that objective in their job.

It is trying for individuals to have confidence in a thought or perspective on the off chance that their chief isn't additionally dedicated to the vision and enabling their representatives or devotees to make a fitting move. At the point when you show others how its done, your devotees ought to see that you are sure and committed, and they will need to adjust their way of behaving to their chief.

2. Authority is about individuals.

Conveying and drawing in with your group is fundamental for authority. Relational and relational abilities are vital for any pioneer. Without having the option to convey your vision to other people, initiative will challenge. As a pioneer, you ought to have the most ideal relationship with every colleague. This implies not just connecting with those individuals in high level administration yet in addition individuals who work in the least level positions and in the middle between.

Pioneers ought to attempt to continually further develop connections, their relational abilities and how they impact individuals who encompass them.

3. Center around change.

Change ought to be at the groundwork of each and every authority plan. Individuals need to comprehend what your objectives and goals are and the part they can play in changing the association. When they know

the heading and changes that need to occur, they might be more able to pursue them.
At the point when you urge others to change and develop, you will do likewise as a pioneer. Improve ought to be your concentration, not simply making changes for monetary profit. Center around the general vision and have the desire to achieve change.

4. Be human and concede botches.
No one's perfect, however it tends to be useful so that others could see a pioneer recognize their missteps as it can assist them with being more interesting. Slip-ups can show you how you veered off-track and how you can work on from here on out. A savvy chief gains from each insight and utilizations it to show their representatives and themselves what regions they need to zero in on to develop as an association.
Individuals can lose confidence in others when they are reluctant to acknowledge liability. At the point when a pioneer possesses a misstep, they are many times held in higher respect.

5. Grasp the benefit of tuning in.
Figure out how to listen more than you talk. At the point when you tune in, you could be figuring out important, new data that might

be useful to you lead actually. Pioneers are extraordinary audience members, which doesn't imply that they should concur with all that they hear, yet they should attempt to figure out it and comprehend.

There are two degrees of human grasping: scholarly and close to home. At the point when you comprehend what somebody is talking about, this is the scholarly level. The close to home degree of understanding implies that you know how they are feeling. A decent pioneer ought to comprehend both. Individuals feel esteemed and regarded when a pioneer carves out opportunity to tune in and process what they are talking about.

6. Foster initiative abilities.

A pioneer is characterized by their way of behaving and activities, and a decent pioneer has explicit abilities and qualities that assist them with driving successfully.

To be an extraordinary pioneer, you ought to perceive the abilities you really want and attempt to foster them. Distinguish your assets and shortcomings and what your administration technique will be. You really want to figure out your own ways of behaving and perspectives, and what these mean for your capacity to lead. You should continually chip away at your abilities and consistently endeavor to further develop them since they decide how fruitful your authority style will be.

7. Advance variety.

A pioneer ought to invite variety and saddle the qualities that it can give on an organization. At the point when everybody has a similar foundation and experience, it implies there is a restricted main subject area, however when there is an assorted reach, you might have the option to move toward things diversely and track down new viewpoints.

A different labor force supports development and novel thoughts, which thusly improves the probability of progress. Many ways of thinking currently distinguish variety as key to business achievements like benefit and development. A pioneer needs to perceive the significance of variety and intend to construct groups that embrace it.

8. Cooperate to accomplish more.

Joint effort is the demonstration of working with others to share data, systems and triumphs, and each extraordinary pioneer grasps its significance. Participation and coordinated effort can occur between associations without influencing solid contest. A pioneer ought to embrace the advantages working cooperatively can bring.

9. Have strong qualities.

A successful pioneer should have a reasonable vision and strong qualities so they can move their supporters and inspire them. Values are fundamental, and they show that you are a believable pioneer. Benefit is crucial for each business, yet it ought not be the sole worth that a pioneer pursues. Representatives value working inside an incredible group, having adaptable working hours, professional stability, preparing and improvement, a happy with workplace and a task that causes them to feel like they are having an effect. Individuals normally need to work with a their pioneer values and needs and has legitimate qualities they follow themselves.

10. Use innovation and advancement.

Since innovation use in the work environment is broad, as a pioneer you ought to exploit the advantages that innovation can bring to your association. Innovation can help in the activity of a business, increment efficiency, help development into new business sectors and work with in accomplishing the organization vision.

Correspondence across the world is simpler utilizing new innovations, which assists with joint effort. Groups can now cooperate regardless of whether they are situated in various nations.

It is fundamental to solid authority that you comprehend and teach yourself on the advances that are engaged with your association. You can then develop how they are utilized so you gain the most advantage. It is additionally fundamental to comprehend what challenges there could be and the way that you can conquer them. Your vision for the future could be impacted by the innovation that is accessible or by future advancements.

11. Help to foster future pioneers.

There is generally a requirement for good initiative, and part of being an extraordinary pioneer is to ensure there is another person who can assume control over your job when essential. Pondering the future in this manner is areas of strength for a quality. The association will profit from having an arrangement set up that leaves no delay when individuals have no pioneer to look to. At the point when representatives are instructed on the most proficient method to become pioneers, they are inspired to take responsibility for work.

Pioneers ought to comprehend the worth of instruction and the improvement of ranges of abilities, support ability inside the labor force and have the option to distinguish and coach the people who could become heads representing things to come

Chapter 4
Principle of Reputation

Anything worth structure merits securing. An organization's standing is its most important resource and should be secured.

An organization's standing is worked over the long run. A decent standing is based on uprightness, trust, and genuineness. Representatives and clients just hear half of what an organization says, yet encounters all that an organization does or doesn't do. An organization's standing will either make them or break them. It takes the dominance five principles of business to fabricate and keep a decent standing and business picture. Nonetheless, it doesn't take a lot to obliterate an organization notoriety or picture.

An organization can't fabricate a standing on the thing they will do, just on what they do or don't do.

Warren Buffett says all that needs to be said, "It requires 20 years to fabricate a standing and five minutes to demolish it. That's what assuming you ponder, you'll do things another way."

It is a lot simpler, requires not so much investment but rather more practical to construct and keep a decent business notoriety than it is to attempt to fix a discolored one. Ordinarily once a business picture has been discolored, it can never recuperate.

An organization's standing influences development and income. It's essential to keep a remarkable standing to draw in and keep clients as well as representatives. Realizing what influences an organization's standing and the way that you can work on the standing of your organization can assist with achieving your extension objectives, lay out your image and increment your deals. In this article, we make sense of what an organization's standing is, the reason it's significant and examine what elements can affect an organization's standing, with tips to further develop how the general population sees your business.

Update your resume

Exhibit your abilities with assistance from a resume master

What is an organization notoriety?

An organization's standing is a public view of the organization and how it works. This remembers popular feelings for the organization's items or administrations or how the organization treats its workers. A standing can be positive or negative, and it can change over the long run. For instance, a famous report about an organization can change its standing, however so can verbal exchange among clients of the business. Since an organization's standing is constrained by customers' insights, it may not necessarily in all cases reflect how the business works. It's critical that the organization deals with its standing to precisely mirror the business.

For what reason is a positive organization notoriety significant?

A positive organization notoriety is significant on the grounds that it can assist your business with developing. Checking the assessments of your clients keeps up with your standing. At the point when clients and potential clients have an uplifting perspective on your organization, they're bound to keep on belittling your business. They're additionally bound to feel much better about supporting your business and to enlighten others regarding their experience. This can all bring about bigger benefits and expanded achievement.

What elements influence an organization notoriety?

Here are a few factors that can influence an organization's standing:

Client care

Client support can generally affect your organization's standing. Clients who have a positive involvement in your organization and the staff who give client support are bound to do rehash business with you. They're additionally bound to educate others regarding their experience, which can expand your client base. In any case, one negative communication can influence your standing, so it's essential to give a reliably sure client care insight.

Item or administration quality

The nature of your item or administration, including how safe it is, can influence your organization's standing. Assuming your client care is perfect and the nature of your items

or administrations dazzles your clients, they'll feel that your administration matches the nature of what you're selling. This can enormously build your positive standing. Making a top notch item or administration that clients worth can likewise assist with expanding income and grow your client base.
Promoting
Promoting is a way your organization speaks with customers and can immensely affect your organization's standing. In the event that your organization's standing isn't so sure as you believe it should be, you can involve promoting as a device to further develop it. Promoting procedures, for example, a brand crusade, can assist with working on an organization's standing. For instance, brand crusades try to increment brand perceivability and impacts customers' perspectives on your organization. The substance you must impart to clients is steady and mirrors the upsides of your organization.
Representative treatment
Making a positive encounter for your representatives can be basically as significant as making one for clients. Assuming representatives appreciate

working at your conversation, this can impact their work and increment quality and efficiency. Worker fulfillment and their perspectives on your organization likewise impact how clients feel. At the point when representatives love to work at your organization, clients can accept that your organization has great qualities and thinks often about individuals over benefits. You can guarantee an extraordinary representative encounter by offering benefits and requesting input from workers to assist with further developing the workplace.

Monetary execution

A decent monetary presentation gives validity to your organization and influences its standing. Frequently buyers see monetary accomplishment as a marker that it's an incredible organization with quality labor and products. Contrarily, in the event that your organization isn't monetarily fruitful, shoppers might be less certain about their decision to put resources into your organization by buying items. Your monetary presentation can give understanding to purchasers about how effectively the business works and what the organization culture might be like, which can impact their perspectives on the organization. Monetary achievement helps your organization in numerous ways, one of which is giving a positive standing.

Ecological effect

The effect your organization has on the climate matters to buyers and can influence your organization's standing in a positive or negative manner. You can show social obligation by restricting the natural impact your organization has. For instance, you can present a reusing program in your organization to diminish waste and play it safe while discarding unsafe or hazardous substances. Being an earth inner voice organization can gain you appreciation and deference from buyers which decidedly affects your standing.

Corporate culture

Corporate culture is an assumption for ways of behaving inside the organization for representative associations and outside business collaboration. This influences the recruiting system, worker maintenance, correspondence and the executives.

Corporate culture can empower superior execution when your organization recruits representatives whose values line up with the organization culture. Your organization's association remotely can accompany different organizations or networks. It's critical to cultivate significant connections and this can assist with acquiring a brilliant standing.

Magnanimous endeavors

Your organization's standing can work on through magnanimous endeavors. Being magnanimous as an organization and advancing general government assistance towards others energizes a positive insight. The generous endeavors of your organization likewise assist with building connections and lay out entrust with clients, which can expand dependability and income for your organization. Charity can likewise lift confidence level sums representatives and draw in ability to your labor force. Giving to good cause, participating in gift matching projects and beginning drives to help in networks are ways your organization can expand its altruistic endeavors.

Client protection

Clients esteem their security and they should trust your organization to safeguard their data. This incorporates sharing their location, name, buy history and installment data.

Security influences your image and your organization's standing. It's a moral practice to keep client data hidden and buyers value organizations that treat moral obligation in a serious way. Keeping up with client security can give an upper hand over different organizations that might share or sell client data. You can rather build your incomes by offering clients security and acquiring their reliability

Chapter 5
Principle of Consistency

Consistency fabricates believability. Validity permits a business to encounter life span. Consistency in business isn't a choice, making progress is fundamental. Irregularity comes from an absence of surveying, distinguishing, planning, creating, and executing. One method for guaranteeing consistency is through arrangements and systems. Anything that should be accomplished at least a couple of times needs a methodology or it won't be done likewise without fail.

Consistency begins with the initiative of an organization. At the point when the administration comprehends the significance of consistency in all they say and do, they will

then show others how its done concerning consistency and enable others to do likewise.
Irregularities in a business will:
Sabotage credibility,
Foster confusion,
Breakdown trust,
Destroy an organizations reputation,
Eventually shut an organization down.
Consistency in a business will:
Make credibility
Foster trust and reliability
Build an unmistakable and conspicuous business picture and brand
Build a decent organization reputation
Retain current clients
Bring a wealth of references, new business with less cost
Longevity in business
Consistency may simply be the contrast among progress and disappointment. Maintaining an effective business can be troublesome, however on the off chance that you center around being predictable in your everyday business, you will make more progress in your endeavors. Consistency will be the way to accomplishing your objectives, regardless of what objective you go for. This is the way to foster compelling systems to

assist you with becoming reliable in your endeavors and results

Consistency brings esteem through laying out trust, which thusly prompts better client support, more noteworthy consumer loyalty, and more trust in achieving security. It begins with you as a business person: Consistency is the means by which you plan, not what you plan. At the point when individuals are steady in specific things, it turns into a propensity and it makes major areas of strength for a between what's going on and the way things are arranged, and when you fabricate a predictable relationship with your representatives, clients, accomplices, and others in your business, this propensity turns into a strong starting point for the drawn out progress and development of their business. Many elements add to the progress of your image, yet maybe one of the most significant is the consistency of content. The nature of content and when you distribute it is additionally a fundamental piece of a clever promoting methodology. Whether you blog consistently or one time each week, it's critical that your association picks a timetable. On the off chance that your substance isn't steady in quality, amount, or timetable, it will confound clients. Adherence to customary systems adds to a superior client experience and fabricates validity, notoriety, and brand trust.

The manner in which your association looks, sounds, and works straightforwardly impacts how current and future clients see your organization. Your image is your most significant resource since it is customized to your business. When you have a delivery plan with your clients, you can utilize Google Analytics to screen and track your presentation to see when commitment is high and when it is low.

By following numerous measurements, including the time spent on each page, you can deal with your distributions each day, week, and month better and all the more actually. You can start this interaction by posting content at specific times or on substituting days. A similar strategy can likewise be utilized with Google Analytics and Facebook to follow your investigation via virtual entertainment stages.

Customary distributions likewise give the chance to gain from clients, and in the event that you are keen on realizing what they need, content creation turns into a

straightforward matter.
Utilize a stage like Google Analytics to screen the main exhibition pointers for your blog. You might need to follow skip rates to check whether clients are leaving your site without taking any kind of action or visiting another site. You will likewise need to follow site visits on the blog to recognize the points that resound most with your crowd.

Conclusion:
Your business needs Vision, Discernment, Leadership, Reputation and Consistency to grow.
Never underestimate the power of these principles and always apply them in your business.
It would help you achieve a better and greater result.

www.ingramcontent.com/pod-product-compliance
Lightning Source LLC
Chambersburg PA
CBHW050326220526
45465CB00005B/2156